1 MONTH OF
FREE
READING

at

www.ForgottenBooks.com

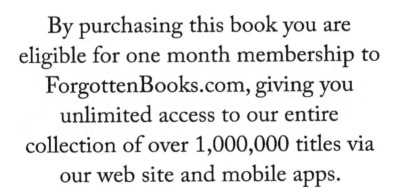

By purchasing this book you are eligible for one month membership to ForgottenBooks.com, giving you unlimited access to our entire collection of over 1,000,000 titles via our web site and mobile apps.

To claim your free month visit:

www.forgottenbooks.com/free93302

ISBN 978-0-483-41601-7
PIBN 10093302

Manuals of Faith and Duty.

EDITED BY REV. J. S. CANTWELL, D.D.

A SERIES of short books in exposition of prominent teachings of the UNIVERSALIST CHURCH, and the moral and religious obligations of believers. They are prepared by writers selected for their ability to present in brief compass an instructive and helpful Manual on the subject undertaken. The volumes will be affirmative and constructive in statement, avoiding controversy, while specifically unfolding doctrines.

The MANUALS OF FAITH AND DUTY are issued at intervals of three or four months; uniform in size, style, and price.

No. I.
THE FATHERHOOD OF GOD.
By Rev. J. COLEMAN ADAMS, D.D., Chicago.

No. II.
JESUS THE CHRIST.
By Rev. S. CRANE, D.D., Norwalk, O.

No. III.
REVELATION.
By Rev. I. M. ATWOOD, D.D., President of the Theological School, Canton, N. Y.

No. IV.
CHRIST IN THE LIFE.
By Rev. WARREN S. WOODBRIDGE, Adams, Mass.

Among the subjects and writers already selected are: "Retribution," by Rev. J. M. Pullman, D.D., and "The Birth from Above," by Rev. Charles F. Lee. Other volumes and writers will be announced hereafter.

PUBLISHED BY THE

UNIVERSALIST PUBLISHING HOUSE,
BOSTON, MASS.
Western Branch: 69 Dearborn Street, Chicago.

𝕸anuals of 𝕱aith and 𝕯uty.

No. IV.

CHRIST IN THE LIFE.

BY

REV. WARREN S. WOODBRIDGE.

"I AM COME THAT THEY MIGHT HAVE LIFE, AND THAT THEY
MIGHT HAVE IT MORE ABUNDANTLY."

John x. 10.

BOSTON:

UNIVERSALIST PUBLISHING HOUSE.

1889.

Manuals of Faith and Duty.

EDITED BY REV. J. S. CANTWELL, D.D.

A SERIES of short books in exposition of prominent teachings of the UNIVERSALIST CHURCH, and the moral and religious obligations of believers. They are prepared by writers selected for their ability to present in brief compass an instructive and helpful Manual on the subject undertaken. The volumes will be affirmative and constructive in statement, avoiding controversy, while specifically unfolding doctrines.

The MANUALS OF FAITH AND DUTY are issued at intervals of three or four months; uniform in size, style, and price.

No. I.
THE FATHERHOOD OF GOD.
By Rev. J. COLEMAN ADAMS, D.D., Chicago.

No. II.
JESUS THE CHRIST.
By Rev. S. CRANE, D.D., Norwalk, O.

No. III.
REVELATION.
By Rev. I. M. ATWOOD, D.D., President of the Theological School, Canton, N. Y.

No. IV.
CHRIST IN THE LIFE.
By Rev. WARREN S. WOODBRIDGE, Adams, Mass.

Among the subjects and writers already selected are: "Retribution," by Rev. J. M. Pullman, D.D., and "The Birth from Above," by Rev. Charles F. Lee. Other volumes and writers will be announced hereafter.

PUBLISHED BY THE
UNIVERSALIST PUBLISHING HOUSE,
BOSTON, MASS.
Western Branch: 69 Dearborn Street, Chicago.

Manuals of Faith and Duty.

No. IV.

CHRIST IN THE LIFE.

BY

REV. WARREN S. WOODBRIDGE.

I)

"I AM COME THAT THEY MIGHT HAVE LIFE, AND THAT THEY
MIGHT HAVE IT MORE ABUNDANTLY."

John x. 10.

BOSTON:

UNIVERSALIST PUBLISHING HOUSE.

1889.

University Press:
John Wilson and Son, Cambridge.

A vital force lies back of all the growth of human character, as it lies back of all growth of the external world. And as the countless lilies of the field confess to one common, pervading vital force, so the leaves of the tree of life, the branches of the true vine, are the organic outgrowth of the same principle. This common, pervading life is Christ.

PROF. J. L. DIMAN.

CHRIST IN THE LIFE.

THE theme assigned to this number of the "Manuals of Faith and Duty" has definite limits. Of necessity each writer is confined to the most condensed treatment of a particular phase of Christian faith and duty. The object of this volume is to exhibit Christ in the life of man. In the treatment two courses are open. One might attempt an exhaustive and profound essay from a metaphysical standpoint, dealing with the deeper problems of the soul; or he might sketch the workings of Christ in the life in their more external aspects, keeping all the time near the daily walk and conversation of men. To adopt either one of these methods exclusively, would be to fail to meet the requirements of the book. It is not designed to be a metaphysical essay, and yet it is hoped it will not prove a superficial treatment of the theme. The great aim, however, will be to be practical. The governing purpose will be to make helpful suggestions. The movement will be along familiar lines. The intent is ever to keep close to the life of men, and to point the way by which the Christ life may be brought more abundantly into human hearts.

I. — HISTORICAL REALITY OF THE CHRIST.

We must be impressed, first of all, with the fact that *the Christ is.* We have had already in this series a volume on " Jesus the Christ," — a statement of what He is.[1] For the purpose of this volume we only ask that the fact that the Christ *is* be laid hold upon. Some say, the Christ has been. Some say, He is yet to come in His greatest power. His existence is not only a past fact, but a present one. We have full knowledge of the Christ from the New Testament record. The story is inspiring. We may and do feed upon it. We have also knowledge of the Christ in Christian institutions. The Church bears witness of the Christ. The Lord's

[1] Manuals of Faith and Duty, No. II., by Rev. Stephen Crane, D.D.

Supper testifies of Him. The book, then, is not all. Nor is the Christ's life confined to three decades of the world's history. The Christ, in Christian institutions and in spirit, continues to be in the life of the world. We must not make Him remote and unreal. He speaks not only the Palestinian word, which comes full of life down the ages, but He also speaks into the hearts and souls of men in this hour. This is the " age to come," the era of the Christ. It *now is* the time which floated before the vision of the prophet, as with uplifted soul he was impressed with divine truth. It is the " great and notable day of the Lord." " A king reigns and prospers, and executes justice and judgment in the earth." [1] " The spirit of the Lord hath rested " upon one, " the spirit of wisdom and understanding, the spirit of counsel and might, the spirit of knowledge and of the fear of the Lord." [2] The one anointed " to preach good tidings unto the meek," sent " to bind up the broken-hearted, to proclaim liberty to the captives, and the opening of the prison to them that are bound ; to proclaim the acceptable year of the Lord, and the day of vengeance of our God ;

[1] Jeremiah xxiii. 5.　　　[2] Isaiah xi. 2.

to comfort all that mourn,"[1]—this one has come and is with us. Though in bodily and visible presence His days on earth were few, and we are separated from that period by the intervening centuries, yet in a most deep and practical sense we ought to say and feel that He *is*, and not that He has been. We do not want to look across the gulf of years. We want the Christ with us here and now. This is the era of the Christ. "It is the last time."[2] The age to come has come; and there is no other age provided for in the economy of God, or revealed in His word.

II.—HINDRANCES TO CHRIST'S WORK IN THE LIFE.

But there are hindrances to Christ's work in the life. There are antichrists. Though the Christ is, He may not have entered your heart or mine; He may not have touched our lives; He may not have reached us with His help and power. Current theology has it that we are fallen in Adam, prone to evil, averse to good. There is no doubt of a hereditary taint, of an existent moral corruption and tendency to evil.

---

[1] Isaiah lxi. 1–3.   [2] 1 John ii. 18.

The Gospel sums up these tendencies, and calls them, in one comprehensive term, " the world ; " no doubt because in fact there was in Christ and the disciples a spirit and life sharply contrasted with the spirit and life of all the world beside. This same tendency is called in the individual " the flesh." The evil, sinful life is the carnal, the fleshly life. And, further, this proneness to evil is projected into another form, is personified and called " the devil." " The world, the flesh, and the devil " are one and the same thing in different aspects. They are names for all corruption or corrupting influences, viewed now as one whole existent in the world and opposed to the spirit of Christ, now as working in the individual life, and again vividly as having a separate and personal being and name. We have not yet reached a point where we may drop the terms " the world, the flesh, and the devil." These words have not lost their original force, nor have the tendencies for which they stand ceased to be. The roots of sin are the same in all ages. The occasions of sin vary with the times.

What are the corrupting tendencies of to-day? What do we find when we make search for the things that are opposed to the Christ, and keep His spirit out of our lives? Saint John tersely defined sin as "the transgression of the law." [1] We want to know something of the temptations, the motives, the inducements that invite to the transgression of the law. The question presents itself in practical form in this wise: Why is there so large a proportion of grasping selfishness, so much indirection and dishonesty, so much that is brutal and repulsive and unlovely in life? What hinders the coming in of those graces and virtues of the Christian life, so admirable and so attractive? As we look for an answer we shall find the causes partly in the already corrupted and weakened spirit of man, and partly in the outward circumstances that minister to his depravity.

Man is, as theology has said, "prone to evil." He is also, as theology has neglected to say, prone to good; that is, he is a free and finite being, with mixed motives and an imperfect character. He has power to choose the evil, and power to choose the good. Of himself he stands ever at the parting of two roads. He may take the strait and narrow path that leads

[1] 1 John iii. 4.

to life, or the broad way that leads to moral
ruin. Each passing day opens such an opportunity, offers such a privilege, brings such a
responsibility. The decision of this hour has
an effect upon the decision of the next. The
choice of the right to-day makes easier and
more likely the choice of the right to-morrow.
The choice of the wrong to-day makes easier and
more likely the choice of the wrong to-morrow.
Each repetition of right choice intrenches one
against wrong choice. Each repetition of wrong
choice intrenches one against right choice.
And were it not for God and His ministration
through Christ, one might become hopelessly
fixed in the love and choice of evil. Under the
working of this divine law, we find ourselves in
the condition which Saint Paul so vividly describes. Will is weakened; motive is wanting.
It is easiest to choose the wrong. We have to
struggle against the weakness caused either by
our own habit or the habit of our ancestry.
When we are in such condition, when we more
easily and more often choose the wrong, we can
say with Saint Paul, " Sin dwelleth in me." [1]
We then find a law that when we would do good

[1] Romans vii. 20.

evil is present with us.[1]   And when, in our better moments, we delight in the law of the Lord,
and find that other law warring against the law
of God, then it does seem to be not us, but sin
that dwelleth in us, by which we are provoked
to evil works.   The struggle seems to be, and
may well be described as, a warfare between
ourselves and sin; and it does seem that sin
has a strength and form and existence of its
own.   It is in reality a warfare between our
better, higher selves and ourselves down at the
lower levels; a struggle between our nobler in-
stincts and our baser passions, between our
higher thought and conscience and our weakened will and perverted desire.   The good that
we would we do not, but the evil that we would
not that we do.[2]   Under this law one may rise
or fall in spiritual life and moral strength.
One's resistance to evil may become weaker
and weaker.   The struggle to human eyes may
seem altogether to have ceased.   One may drop
below the point of making any contest against
sin, below the point of appreciating Saint Paul's
meditations.   One may so habitually choose the
evil and live in it, that there will be no more

----

[1] Romans vii. 21.   [2] Ibid. vii. 19.

than fitful and momentary thoughts of the good; he may become hardened and rebellious, or utterly careless and indifferent. This is the awfulness of sin. "If the light that is in thee be darkness, how great is that darkness!" [1] Thus is built up the highest barrier against the incoming of Christ into the heart. But it is not insurmountable. The infinite God out of His infinite love has sent the Lord Jesus Christ "to seek and *to save* that which was lost." [2] But we need fully to realize that every step away from the Christ counts one on the return. Every step downward means an added measure to the journey upward. And not only so, but with each downward step we acquire a momentum on the downward way. One step away from the Christ may mean many more before we can be recalled, and multiplied hardships on the return. This is a fact of gravest importance. This makes each moment a precious moment and of supreme importance. It attaches to every passing hour all that splendid and awful significance which current theology has attached only to one experience and one crisis in the life.

[1] Matthew vi. 23.   [2] Luke xix. 10.

The roots of sin, then, are in the moral make-up of man. Why he is morally made up as he is, is not here to be discussed. As a matter of fact man's splendid gift of freedom involves a great danger. We find it true that he has not faćed the peril in safety. We find him weak and prone to err. We find his moral weakness a hindrance to the building up of his life into the Christlikeness.

III. — The Antichrists of Society and the Age.

Now we consider the external phases of the hindrances of the Christ's helpful work in the life. What are the occasions of sin?

This brings us into practical contact with our time. It leads us to look at the life of to-day, to note what is unfavorable to the promotion of Christian virtue, what circumstances favor the breeding of evil, and what invites the transgression of the spiritual and moral law.

The inquiry is of such proportions, and our space is so limited that we must sketch and condense, or make choice of some phase of the subject and enlarge upon that. We shall find it more profitable to neglect the more obvious occasions of transgression which are concerned with the grosser forms of sin. There is scarcely need to mention the nurseries of vice and crime, or to tell the appalling story of gross evil and wickedness fostered in centres where the vile and low are wont to congregate. It is enough to say that these horrible occasions of sin do exist; that once the will is weakened, once the passions gain the mastery, once evil appetites are aroused, then one has to take but a step, and he will find surroundings which will minister to and foster all that is low and vile within him. These things are open to every one's view. Upon them we often dwell. Rather should our attention be called to less obvious, more subtle, yet scarcely less dangerous occasions of moral weakness. We are making the mistake in this age of observing the moral disease of man only at its height; we grow desperate over the last stages, and you will hear men crying out that some one great evil is the cause of all other evils; we are less concerned about the thousand little things that make possible the great thing; we are blind to the conditions that lead to the inception of the disease; we treat the disease; we neglect moral sanitation; we treat the fever

at its height, in its epidemic rage; we neglect
the generally weakened condition of the people
which made it possible for the disease to get
its hold; we do not take sufficient note of the
thousand contributing causes which *must be
dealt with* before the disease can be rooted out.

Whatever the original cause (and that is perhaps beyond our ken), it is a fact that certain
of the modern conditions and habits, certain of
the phases of modern civilization, have in them
the seeds of moral weakness; under them without forethought and effort we are bound to become weakened, and at last must come into such
condition that every shape of moral disease can
fasten upon us.

The commercial and industrial, the wealth-
getting habit of the age is one of these phases.
A larger proportion of man's energy is absorbed
in these directions than ever before. It is an
eminently materialistic age. The things of the
spirit have less emphasis, the things of the
earth have more emphasis, than makes a goodly
proportion. Reach out your hand indifferently
to-day, and you will be more apt to touch something that savors of the earth than something
that savors of the spirit. The air is more

saturated with materialistic than with spiritual
substance. It is easier to hear and learn of the
factory, of the farm, of stocks, bonds, ships, and
trade, than of honor, virtue, and godliness. A
great wheat-deal has a wider reach and more
points of immediate contact with the life of the
people than the discussion in the American
Board of the most momentous spiritual problems.
We breathe in with every breath the air of the
shop and the counting-room ; only now and
then comes a draught of the spirit from the
Prophets and the Christ. Our young men grow
up in the atmosphere of trade ; the thoughts
and sentiments, the ambitions and desires, of the
commercial world are their daily sustenance ;
only now and then have they a taste of the true
bread that cometh down from Heaven. Our
young women grow up in secular surroundings ;
their devotions are more easily and naturally
turned to material things than to the culture
of the spiritual life. The channels for the out-
flow of the energy in secular directions open up
on every hand, and are kept free and attractive ;
and *into these channels goes by far the larger proportion of the splendid strength of the human soul.*

Another unpleasant sign of the secular and

unspiritual characteristic of the age appears in the devotion of the people to pure amusement. Hard work and energy-draining diversion are characteristic of the American people; recreation has come to be an added business. The man who in addition to his regular occupation meets all the demands of society must be very strong; and if above meeting the demands of business and society he would meet his obligations to the Church, he must be extraordinarily robust. The devotion of our people to pure diversion is a sign of the times. If our average village life may be taken as an epitome of the life of the people, there is a feverish desire on every hand for pure amusement. It is not recreation that is sought; there is no relation of the diversion to health and strength. The indulgence is not temperate and helpful; it indicates an unbalanced and thoughtless life. Amusement has become the secondary occupation of our people, having the first and chief claim after necessary labor; it uses up the winter evenings and the summer days. Surely the present style of life must sometime have an effect upon the character of the people; can we not see the beginnings already? It must gradually, unperceived at first, change the quality of the life; it must have an effect upon the physical, upon the mental, upon the moral, and upon the spiritual fibre of man. Our young people tend to grow up with a passion for pure diversion. The serious duties of life are irksome, and are not undertaken with courage and a cheerful spirit. The home life suffers. Children are not educated in the home as they ought to be; they are not under influences that tend to raise up sturdy, work-loving, burden-bearing men and women. We need not doubt that the coming generations will be good card-players, graceful dancers, patrons of amusement, and capable in every pastime; but we have some reason to be anxious on the score of the strength, the force and quality of character of those who are subject to the prevailing influences of to-day. Are we producing a generation of sturdy, virtue-loving, wise, broad-minded, generous men and women, who will take up family cares with zest and courage, who will put strength of heart and soul and the vigor of strong nerves and a healthy organism and an enduring Christian purpose into the splendid opportunities that everywhere confront the humblest child of God?

No word is here written against recreation. If space permitted, right here would be an essay on recreation which would satisfy the most enthusiastic lover of any legitimate pastime; but any sport, any amusement, any diversion ceases to be a recreation when it acts as a drain upon the energies, when it exhausts rather than restores, when it is pursued with passionate fondness and takes out of the life more than it puts in.

This is a matter of more importance than many are ready to admit. We are swinging too far from Puritanism. Like the Puritans, we are overdoing, but in the opposite direction. They destroyed a part of life by striking out cheerfulness: we are destroying a much more important part of life by striking out seriousness. They were nobly equipped for the sterner tasks: we are splendidly caparisoned for the lighter pleasures. They frowned upon recreation and sport: we frown upon plodding earnestness and the spirit which takes a downright grip upon every serious problem and hardest task. The prevailing fondness for pastime and amusement for their own sakes, and to fill up the hours so that earnestness shall not intrude,

drains off the divine life, that is ever sent down
from heaven to us. This current of life, rich and
pure, comes continually from God. But at point
after point in our careless and indifferent and
worldly life it is conducted off, and dissipated,
and in us becomes enfeebled.

In these aspects of our civilization and life
are presented very serious hindrances to the entrance of Christ into the human heart; in these
shapes antichrist appears. They are the more
dangerous because they are not connected with
what is in itself wrong. Yet they do have a
large and an important place in all that con-
cerns the spiritual and moral welfare of our
people. They are causes of degeneration. They
need to be considered. In these dangers child-
hood and youth are immersed. They are more
serious because so little repulsive. They are
more threatening because everywhere connected
with respectability. They touch the life at every
point. They are operative upon that large class
of people who are independent and intelligent,
sensible in the main, law-abiding, the rank and
file, a substantial set, upon whom we look as the
bulwark of society, the conservators of law, in
whose hands is largely the future of our nation.

Surely anything which endangers the Christian life of this class needs quick attention. For when this great body, which is our hope, degenerates, when it drops down one grade, then indeed is an injury done to the life of the people, and their welfare seriously endangered.

Against the barriers set up by man's moral weakness and by the occasions of sin found in the circumstances of his life, the Christ has to work. The aim of Christian effort is to overcome these obstacles and bring Christ into the life. We proceed to consider, in the next five sections, the instrumentalities or means by which this work may be done.

IV.— HELPFUL INSTRUMENTALITIES.—THE BIBLE.

Roughly summed up, the means, or instrumentalities, or helps toward the Christian life are the Bible, Meditation, Prayer, Family Worship, and the Church.

We proceed to consider, in this section, *the Bible*. It is a potent means whereby the Christ may find entrance into the life. We need to use it. It is a chart of life. It gives knowledge of the greatest events and the grandest men of the world's history. He who is familiar with the Bible, not verbally or with detached texts, but with the sweep of its history, the progress and development of its life, the character of its greatest men, is possessed of an inexhaustible store, whence may be drawn all the riches of life. He who has learned to appreciate its poetry, to have an appetite for its wisdom, to sympathize with its loftiest spirit, to dwell admiringly and lovingly with men like Moses, like Isaiah, like John, like Paul, like the Christ, is feeding upon the meat that makes men godlike. The Bible contains a record of the highest aspirations, of the noblest thoughts, the sublimest sentiments. It tells the story of the strongest, purest life. It leads us into the presence of those who have held communion with God, opens to our view the life of Jesus the Christ. It contains the annals of the founding of the Church, the precious letters of apostolic instruction, and the sublime apocalypse of the triumph and glory of the Church. We must make the Bible our meat and drink. Nowhere else can we to such purpose and so bountifully supply our highest needs. The Bible is not first to be reverenced and then used. It is first to be used and then it must be reverenced. It is not to be made a fetich, an object of worship. It is an instrument, which the Divine order has placed within our reach. If we use it, we shall learn its worth, and love it as we love no other book. It is a book to be used not with the critic's skill and learning, — the order of the history of the pentateuch, the time of the prophets' writing make little difference to the searcher after spiritual food, — but with an honest purpose and an open heart; a book to bring to our notice and to enlarge our power of seeing those sublime truths which are so easily missed in our ordinary life; a book to awaken and develop those finer qualities of heart and soul, which become dulled in the busy turmoil and temptation of daily living; a book to lead us into intimacy with souls who have been acquainted with the highest truth, who have been pure and holy, nay, who have walked with God; and above all, into intimacy with the great Master of them all, the Lord Jesus Christ.

V. — THE HELP OF MEDITATION.

Our reading of the Bible should be supplemented with *meditation*. This is a means of bringing the Christian spirit into the heart. We need "The Still Hour." There are so many demands upon our intelligence, so many uses for the intellect, so many objects of thought, so much to fill the brain and keep it active, that there is little chance in these days for quiet meditation. If we desire it, it is hard to find the still hour. These other demands upon the thought are louder and more obtrusive. The whole outward machinery of our life is adapted to them. The routine of life does not provide for the meditative moment, for the blessed privilege of solitude, for the hour to be spent alone in the presence of the Highest. Once it was different. Long ago, the cloister was of chief importance in the religious life. Then there was too much solitude, too much introspection. The cloistered monks thinned out the life. They fell into vagaries and notions. They passed the bounds of sound mental and spiritual health. They shunned the active world, where they might have relieved the strain of their intense thought and tested and corrected the product of their meditative hours. For them it was all cloister and no world. Now it is all world and no cloister. There is no provision for the meditative hour. Our churches are closed except for regular worship; our shops and marts of course admit of no such thing, and even our homes are busy places. We have to make a special effort to find the opportunity. This we ought to do. We ought at times seriously to turn the current of our thought and feeling Christward and Godward. "You have torn down the cloister, but why have you not erected it in your own hearts? Lo, my brother, if thou wouldst seek out the *still hour*, only a single one every day, and if thou wouldst meditate on the love which called thee into being, which hath overshadowed thee all the days of thy life, . . . this would be to draw near to thy God. Thus wouldst thou take Him by the hand." [1]

VI. — THE VALUE OF PRAYER.

Another means for private or individual use in the culture of the Christian life is *prayer*.

Prayer should be the natural outgrowth of Bible reading and meditation. When our thoughts have been with Moses and the Prophets and the Christ, when we have been feeding upon the Psalms, or Isaiah, or the Sermon on the Mount,

[1] The Still Hour, by Austin Phelps, pp. 135, 136.

we ought to find ourselves in the mood for prayer.
We shall want to follow those spiritually minded
men up to the Father. Prayer is a means of en-
riching, enlarging, and strengthening the life.
Our Lord Himself depended upon prayer. He
had moments of exhaustion, of depletion; and
in those moments, and when He was passing
through some special trial, and when He was
undertaking some great work, He went to God
in prayer.

There is something exceedingly touching and
something very instructive in Jesus' habit of private prayer. It is not ostentatious; it is not for
a spectacle; it is not advertised. But we constantly find Him stealing quietly away from all
companionship and seeking the company of God
in prayer. After those exhausting days of teaching and healing, after the drain upon His life in
the presence of multitudes, the flock without a
shepherd, the loving, the curious, the scoffing,
we find Him seeking the fresh breath of the
mountain air, the loneliness of the wilderness,
and there asking for the presence of God in His
heart.[1] He was praying at His baptism, when
the heaven opened and the Spirit descended and

[1] Matthew xiv. 23; Luke v. 16; vi. 12.

abode upon Him.[1] He prayed before the call of
the disciples.[2] He went up into a mountain to
pray, and was praying at the time of the trans-
figuration and the renewal of the voice from
heaven saying, "This is my Beloved Son."[3] He
prayed before Lazarus was raised from the dead;
He prayed with His disciples when they were
troubled at the darkness that seemed to be set-
tling over them, and the danger that threatened
their beloved Lord.[4] He wrestled in prayer;
He groaned and prayed, and at last received
strength and peace, all through the last days
which culminated in the cross.

We then must pray. We must reinforce our
lives. Prayer enables us to receive Divine truth.
It is our means of communicating with the Divine. Whatever other purpose it serves, the
great value of prayer is that it keeps us close to
God, and brings God into our hearts. We may
ask for other things, — we may ask for material
benefits, we may pray for the coming of the rain;
for the staying of the flood, for the arrest of disease; we may pray for the intercession of God,
the staying of the calamity that impends; and

[1] Luke iii. 21.   [2] Ibid. vi. 12.
[3] Ibid. ix. 28–35.   [4] John xvii.

men who dwell near to God will continue to speak to Him of all their needs, and in simple fashion to express before Him every earnest desire : but in these lines, after all, we do not know whether in folly or in wisdom our prayer ascends, we are very likely to ask amiss and to receive not. We must ask in His name, in His spirit. And surely His prayers were largely for the incoming of the Divine spirit into His soul. When we seek God for the sake of finding *Him*, for the sake of receiving His life, then we cannot be asking amiss, and we must receive. It is best, like Solomon, not to ask for ourselves long lives, or riches, or the lives of our enemies, but for a wise and an understanding heart.[1] We must seek for ourselves first the kingdom of God and His righteousness, and let all other things be added in their proper time and order.[2] Asking this, we shall surely receive. Seeking this, we shall surely find.

Prayer is the hallowed and sacred coming into the Divine presence, asking of God that He bestow His spirit upon us. It is based on the belief that there is store of spiritual reality and of truth and of all wisdom and love in the

---

[1] 1 Kings iii. 5–14.   [2] Matthew vii. 33.

Divine heart. It is our humble and reverential and earnest petition for the renewing of our hearts. In our hours of depletion, when we are weary and exhausted, when we feel that strength and life have gone out of us, we need, like our Lord and Master, to go apart and pray. We need the constant inflow of the Divine spirit, the constant presence of God. We need the Divine strength. We need to be fed from on high; and prayer out of earnest hearts will surely bring God into our lives. It will surely renew us for our labor, and give into our hearts the Divine patience and the Divine wisdom. It will surely enlarge our faith and awaken our love; it will enable us to follow our Lord, to walk as He walked, and to be blessed as He was blessed, in sorrow, in temptation, or in toil.

The Bible, meditation, and prayer are means to the great end we have in consideration; namely, the attainment of the Christian life. These means belong more especially to the individual life, or have been considered in that relation. They are for one's private use in the hours devoted to the building up of the character into Christian grace and strength.

VII. — THE AID OF FAMILY WORSHIP.

But there are other relations than those between each individual and his God. The solitary are set together in families. The family is
a Divine institution. It is evident that God designed the family to be a centre of pure life. It
may become the source of untold blessing. Nothing is more important than to make the home a
training-school for life. There should be instilled
every virtue; there the young should be brought
up to reverence God, to be noble, to be manly
and womanly, to be generous and kind, to be
brave and true, to love honor, to have respect to
righteousness. Private Bible-reading and meditation and prayer do not meet all the requirements of the Christian life. The home furnishes
an added opportunity, and makes a new obliga-
tion. There is no quicker, surer, more constant
means of helpfully reaching the life than through
the sacred relations of the home. Christian fa-
thers and mothers ought to be able to rear Christian children. If they do not, they are held
responsible, not for every failure in result, for
sometimes there may be excuse, but for every neglect, for silence upon the great themes of life, for

indifference with regard to the moral welfare of
children, for neglecting to mention Christ, and
omitting to bring the children to an appreciation of the Christlike life. There should be a
wholesome Christian atmosphere in every home.
There should be some themes of conversation beside those that concern trade, dress, amusements,
accidents, crimes, and the happenings of the day.
We cannot expect strong moral and spiritual life
if there is no more bracing air than that in the
home. Children are growing up without de-
cided home influence. The home is too much
a lodging-place and dining-room ; it is too little
the holy of holies of a loving group joined heart
to heart in deep affection for the purpose of the
highest and strongest life.

Christ and God should be systematically
sought in the home. It is to be feared that they
are systematically neglected. The strong tendency, for two generations at least, has been to
neglect family worship, — to throw down the
home altars. As a means of fostering the Christian life the home altar has a place hardly second to the altar of the sanctuary. We have too
much banished the Christ from home life. We
have come to think that His name is to be seri-

ously heard only at church, or in the Sunday-school, or at the conference meeting. Parents no doubt respect religion, and think that their children should learn something of Christian truth, for the Sunday-schools are filled. But they are inclined to put the responsibility of all religious instruction and spiritual guidance, and it might almost be said of moral influence, upon the church and Sunday-school. Pains are not taken to make the home the centre of religious life. This applies to no particular denomination; it is characteristic of the time. It is a woful mistake. We cannot afford to neglect or to forget the Christ six days in the week. We cannot rightly trust our children to develop in Christian character under the influence of two hours' Sabbath instruction, one half of which is ordinarily beyond their understanding, and the other half liable to be the merest formality of question and answer. The father or mother who expects the child to grow up — or to be built up, as the splendid New-Testament expression is — under the influence of the church service and Sunday-school alone, lacks intelligence, or common-sense, or conscience. Such parents are, to say the least, very heedless; and such heed-

lessness ouches the point of criminal neglect.
Make use, parents and guardians of families, of
the home influence, as a means of cultivating the
Christian life. Begin the day with a common
thought of God; have family prayers; avoid
formalism; put no premium on piety of the type
that touches only the outside of life. Make the
worship healthful, wholesome, cheerful; make it
have some concern with the daily walk and conversation. It should be simple, sincère, and
brief. Some part of the Scripture should be
read. Some good thought from another source
is not out of place; in homes where the spirit
of song is, a hymn may be added, and a prayer
should be said. Once, at least, each day should
the family be united in such service. We have,
perhaps, some natural timidity to overcome,
some old prejudices to break down; but for the
sake of themselves, for the sake of their children, for the sake of coming generations, parents must take the Christian training of children into their own hands; they must build
altars in their homes to the good Father, and
bring the household into the Divine presence
every day.

VIII. — THE CHURCH THE GREAT HELP.

There is yet one other means, — the chief and greatest instrumentality in helping to the Christian life, — namely, the Church.

Whatever of attainment is possible without the Church, the full development of the Christ life can only come with the Church. Our brotherhood extends beyond the limits of blood-relationship. "He hath made of one blood all nations of men for to dwell on all the face of the earth."[1] Sacred as is the home, sacred as are the ties of kindred, there is the greater family, — the one family under the fatherhood of God and the brotherhood of man.

No human life can be perfect in isolation. In the great household of God there must be that centre of Christian influence and life, that union of Christian believers, called the Church. Under the Divine law, indeed by the Divine creation, we belong one to another; and if we try to be Christians belonging only each to himself and individually to God, we must fail. One who holds himself apart from that great means of life and

[1] Acts xvii. 26.

work, the organic union of all believers in Christ, is neglecting one of the divinely appointed ways whereby his own life may be enriched, and despising his opportunity to bestow upon others the gifts that Christ has given to men.

The Church serves the end of bringing the Christ into the life in a fourfold way : —

1. It invites us to a *common worship*. There is much in this. We have spoken of private worship. We need also to worship together. We need the help of the union of spirit with spirit, the joining of soul with soul in common aspirations and purposes. Our common worship reminds us of the fatherhood of God, and that we belong in His household. There is a power in the thought and desire of millions unitedly uplifted to God. There is a potent effect in one's presence in the little assemblies which make the units of the mighty whole. "Where two or three are gathered together in my name, there am I in the midst of them." [1] As the small assemblies feel themselves united in the strength of God, and are knit together to make the mighty aggregate, and worship the same Father in unity of spirit, then the life-blood of the Christ flows

[1] Matthew xviii. 20.

rich and free through the many members of the great body. One who separates himself and tries to live a solitary Christian takes himself away from this strong current of spiritual life. Common worship, worship in union and in unison, calls down abundant blessings and brings the Christ richly into the heart.

2. The Church not only provides for a common worship, but also for *Christian teaching* in the spoken word. It has something for the emotions and sentiments; it provides also for the common study of the Divine truth. We are better fitted for Christian living by this teaching. It is profitable to take unitedly into our thought the problems of life, and together to seek light. The constant and systematic application of Christian principles to all the questions of life is secured through the Church. This is a matter of no small moment. That it has an effect cannot be doubted. For the virtues to be dwelt upon, truth to be praised, Christian love urged, the life and teachings of Jesus gone over again and again, each time in fresh applications, each time in relation to different needs and circumstances, is surely a means of cultivating the Christian life. The spoken word could not be

spared. It is a means of keeping our thought fresh, Christ with us, and our hearts warm and true.

3. The Church further brings the Christ into our lives through the *sacraments*.

Baptism is the seal of belief and the symbol of renewal; it is the solemn consecration of the life in the Christian faith; it is the sign of our entrance into a covenant with God; it is the visible writing down of our pledge to follow faithfully after the Christ; it indicates and in symbol foreshadows the great work that the Christ is to do for us; it points forward to the utter cleansing of the life. Having received the rite, we have made a solemn promise to our Father. In the case of children the promise is made for them in hope, and when they come to years of discretion and intelligence they are invited to ratify the promise and make it for themselves. We have entered into the company of others who have made the same promise, and placed ourselves as near as possible to our Saviour and our God. We have taken our stand where all surroundings are most favorable for our growth in Christian character.

The sacrament of the Lord's Supper is another

help offered by the Church. This calls us into the Christ's presence. It removes the vast separation of years that lie between us and the life of our Lord. It is the symbol of the feeding and nurture of the soul upon the Christ life. To eat His body and drink His blood, means, as He Himself indicates, to receive and inwardly to digest His truth.[1] The Lord's Supper is the most sacred memorial of the Christ. Coming to the feast with a true conception of its meaning, with an appreciation of the privilege offered, prepared by earnest thought and devotion, there is a blessing in this sacrament which brings us very near to our Lord, and makes us feel that He has come and dwelt within our hearts.

4. Again, the Church helps us by its invitation to a *common service.* It takes us out to a common work, makes us " laborers together with God." Not till it has called out our strength in some united effort for the good of men has the Church provided all its ways for helping the Christian life. Nothing is so stimulating and helpful as to join hands for some great and good work. The more it involves earnest effort and the bestowal of Christian love, the better its

[1] John vi. 54, 63.

effect upon the workers. By a common service is meant not every trivial work that is done under church auspices, but only such as have the true Christian quality, that involve real Christian effort, — works of benevolence, of church extension, of reform. If the Church offered no common objects of work to her people, if consecrated energies could not be centred upon common ends, it would soon fall into inactivity and pass on to disintegration. Work is in large measure the promoter of vigor and health. The working church is the living church. The grand service to which an active church invites her people is a constant inspiration and source of life. The earnest effort reacts upon the toiler. None is so well prepared to work to-morrow as he who has worked to-day. None has in him in such full measure the spirit of labor as he who is earnestly at the task. The common service to which the Church invites its members is a source of life. It purifies and strengthens the soul.

Such are the means or instrumentalities by which the Christian life may be cultivated. We may make use of the Bible, of meditation, of prayer, of home training and family devotion,

and of the Church, helping us by its common
worship, its spoken word, the sacraments, and
its common work. It is not for any one to
make a choice of these means, but for *every one
to use them all.* They are indissoluble parts of
one solid whole. They cannot be rightly separated. You cannot choose between them, any
more than you can choose by which rail, the
right hand or the left, you will make your journey across the continent, or whether you will
use the steam-boiler or the propeller in your trip
across the Atlantic. There is vast need of more
consolidated and coherent effort all along the
line ; there is need that we realize that the highest ends cannot be attained till we appreciate and
use the grand system of means that is placed in
our hands.

IX. — OUR CONTACT WITH THE CHRIST.

We have seen that the Christ is ; we know
that He ought to be in the life, and have men-
tioned some of the reasons why He is not there,
and have considered some of the means by which
He may enrich our lives. Assuming that we
have used those means, and that the Christ is
beginning to have some hold upon us, we inquire

now as to the *process* of Christ's work, and to this inquiry devote sections nine and ten.

We assume that there has been that recognition of evil in the life which is called *conviction;* that turning away of the thought and life from evil ways, from indifference and disobedience, which is *repentance;* that surrender of one's self to the new idea and way, which is *conversion;* that consciousness that a new spirit has found lodgment and abiding-place in the life, which is the *new birth,* — these experiences are assumed, and we ask as to the process of the Christ's work on and within the heart.

This is a practical question, because the Christian experience has often had an air of mystery and remoteness. It has come to be a common thought that it is something altogether dissociated from life, having little to do with the here and now, but possibly a very important affair in the hereafter. The experience has been taken unnecessarily out of the grasp of the understanding. The humanities of it have not been sufficiently emphasized. It has been made to have an air of unnaturalness. While it is natural and explicable under the well-known and great laws of life, it has been set off by itself and made strange. An inquiry into the facts, then, is in place.

Jesus describes Himself and His work under various differing figures of speech. Combined they give us the complete notion of Himself and His work. He speaks of Himself as our " example," as our " leader," as a Saviour, as a judge. He describes Himself as " the bread of life," as " the water of life," as " the corner-stone," as " the way and the truth and the life ; " calls Himself " the light of the world." He represents Himself under the figure of " the Vine ; " calls Himself " the door " by which His sheep may go in and out and find pasture, and also " the shepherd," " the good shepherd who giveth his life for the sheep." Some of these descriptions present Christ as standing outside our lives and leading us, and some as entering into our lives and feeding us. The Apostles also speak of Jesus' life and work in terms not uniform. Saint Paul exhorts that the same " mind "[1] be in the Philippian disciples that was in Christ. The writer of the Epistle to the Hebrews calls Jesus " the author and finisher of our faith."[2] Saint Peter says that He left an "example"[3] that the brethren

[1] Philippians ii. 5.   [2] Hebrews xii. 2.   [3] 1 Peter ii. 21.

should follow His steps. Saint Paul calls Jesus
the " one mediator between God and men." [1]
He speaks of the law of the spirit of life in
Him which frees us from the law of sin and
death.[2] He says that in Him we have redemption through His blood.[3] Saint John says that
His blood cleanseth from all sin, " if we walk
in the light as He is in the light." [4] Helpful
suggestions as to the process of Jesus' work are
to be found in Jesus' exhortation, " Abide in
me and I in you;" [5] and in Saint Paul's saying
that the baptized have " put on Christ," [6] and
the seemingly contradictory words in the same
epistle, Christ is " formed within you;" [7] and
in his statement that we are called into fellowship with Christ,[8] and that we are " strengthened
with might by His spirit in the inner man." [9]

It must be confessed that from these words of
Christ and the Apostles one gets no very clear
idea as to method or process. They seem themselves to have made no special effort to explain.
They did not enter into any psychologic discussion. They give us no metaphysics. They use

---

[1] 1 Timothy ii 5.   [2] Romans viii 2   [3] Ephesians i. 7.
[4] 1 John i. 7.   [5] John xv. 4.   [6] Galatians iii. 27.
[7] Ibid. iv. 19.   [8] 1 Corinthians i. 9.   [9] Ephesians iii. 16.

such figures as serve on each particular occasion
the special purpose of that time. But such passages as have been cited and the whole New
Testament history indicate this fact: that the
Christ worked upon and within the lives of the
disciples by personal contact of spirit with spirit,
life with life, under the same law and by the
same processes that govern to-day the influence
of one life over another. How strange it is, this
influence of life upon life! What wonderful
power spirit has upon spirit! What strange
contact of soul with soul, with what wonderful
results, we are witnessing all the time! When
we know the process that communicates the bra-
very of a great captain to the men in the ranks,
or that subdues to the sway of a great intellect
thousands of followers, or sends the sentiments
of one great heart thrilling through multitudes,
then we shall know the process by which the
Christ works in our lives. Somehow, we know
not how, spirit and life pass from heart to heart,
from soul to soul. Somehow one great master
mind may enter into and mould other minds.
One generous heart may fill and warm a thousand others. We may say that it is a mystery,
just as the process of the transfer of sunshine

and soil into the living blade of grass is a mystery; but it is a most palpable fact.

Was not the great Saint Bernard communicating himself to the great multitudes that waited upon his words? Were not the hearers who flocked to him from all over Europe receiving himself into their lives? Did he not become a part of them? His remarkable intellect, his simple and sincere piety, his marvellous wisdom were imparted to them. He was in contact with many: the common people heard him in crowds. He was counsellor of kings and nobles, bishops and popes. He ruled Europe by the power of his spirit. That he entered into the hearts of others and gave them his spirit, let the one hundred and sixty populous monasteries formed after his suggestion testify, let the crusade instigated by him bear witness, let the potentates and people of Europe who bowed before him declare. His glowing spirit, his passionate earnestness found its way into other lives.

When King Henry of Navarre rode up and down the lines before the battle of Ivry giving words of encouragement to his soldiers, assuring them that he would either conquer or die, did he not impart something of himself to the waiting army ? " If my standard fail you," said he, " keep my plume in sight. You will always see it in the face of glory and honor." Was not the king living within that army ? Was not he himself, his courage, his purpose, his very life, communicated to them ? The three white plumes of his helmet seen everywhere in the thickest of the fight carried his own valor and spirit into his hosts. Those soldiers trusted him ; they had faith in him. He had faith in them and trusted them. He was in them and they in him. One life can and does fill other lives. One intellect can transform other intellects. One heart can kindle sentiment in other hearts. There is vital union between person and person. A leader, be he theologian, or statesman, or warrior, or philanthropist, or reformer, reproduces himself in his followers. It is a law of the human soul that it can be mightily moved by some other soul. Under that law we live, and move, and have our being. We are ever feeling the power of some other over us, or our power over some other.

Under this law, whose operation is so familiar a fact, the Christ enters into our lives. The spirit that lives in him is the Divine spirit. " I and my Father are one,"[1] He says; "I am in the Father and the Father in me."[2] That spirit which is in Him enters into His disciples; it fills and controls them; it rules and sways their lives. The New Testament picture of apostolic discipleship is a grand picture of lives utterly possessed with the spirit of the Christ. The Christ is in them; His purposes are in them; His motives are in them; His life is in them. "Nevertheless not I live, but Christ liveth in me,"[3] exclaims Saint Paul. Those men had Christ in their hearts. He led them and commanded them from within, and sent them forth in the power of His spirit to do His work. In the same way the spirit of the Christ may work in all men. His spirit touches our spirit. When John Wesley had been preaching for some years he was reconverted, or as he thought for the first time really converted, to Christ. It put new life into him; it awakened every latent power. It sent him forth on that splendid career of consecrated and successful effort which brought forth such abundant fruit, and entitles him to be enrolled among the holy men of God who have turned the currents of the world's life. The

---

[1] John x. 30.   [2] John xiv. 10.   [3] Galatians ii. 20.

Christ-spirit came to him at that time in larger measure; it filled full his soul; he was a new man in Christ. He too might say, "Nevertheless not I live, but Christ liveth in me."

We stand in awe before the complete possession of the human soul by the spirit of the Christ. This utter giving up of the life to another life, and that the life of God as it is in Christ, is a fact of sublime meaning and importance. But the process is just as simple and natural as the way in which the life of a beloved friend finds its way into one's heart. We are kindred spirits with the Christ; we are made in the Divine image. We are sons of God, wayward it is true, strayed away, and needing through Christ to be adopted again into the home,[1] and yet always related to God as children, and to Christ as our elder brother. If we were not divinely created, Christ could not come near us. If we were of some other order, Christ could not enter our lives. If there be mystery about this relation of the Christ with us, it is the same mystery that attaches to the relation of your life with the life of your dear friend. It is not a mystery belonging to the Christ and reli-

---

[1] See "Manuals of Faith and Duty," No. 1, sec. v.

gion, not a mystery that sets Him afar off and separates religion from the understanding, but a mystery that belongs to life itself, and one that we face every day. As your beloved friend finds a way into your heart, and has the power to give you his spirit; so you may come under the spell of the Christ, and find Him filling all your life. You are filled with His motive; His purposes are your purposes; His spirit is your spirit. You cherish and obey Him; you follow Him into all the battle of life; you make struggle with Him against all selfishness and sin; you share His divine enthusiasm; you enter into all that life of love and good-will, of personal purity and righteousness, which means your redemption and the redemption of the world. He is all in all to you; you do not live, but the Christ lives in you.

X. — CHRISTIAN GROWTH.

But we may gather from New Testament teachings something further and more definite with regard to the process of Christ's work.

Sometimes the Christian experience stops with the awakening of the emotions. Christ comes and fills the heart, but for the moment only.

His spirit enters a multitude under some special stress, and thrills them with ecstasy. But the splendid inflow of feeling dies away with the occasion. It is as though the hosts of King Henry, having won the battle of Ivry, and lost sight of their beloved commander for a time, should have melted away and become unavailable for the contests that remained. But this is not New Testament Christianity; this is not the Pauline idea of the Christian life. There must be something besides the momentary presence of the Christ with us. He must not only enter our lives, but He must remain there; He must become assimilated, a part of our very selves. It is a pleasure to eat, and having eaten properly, and being in health, there is a certain satisfaction attending the fact of an appeased hunger. But this pleasure is one of the least of the benefits of eating. It is the digestion of the food, its entrance into the blood, and through the blood into the life, — into all the avenues of activity, promoting health, giving power, and securing growth, — that does the real and abiding good. So it is a pleasure to be deeply moved by the presence of the Christ-spirit. Such emotions give us the highest joy. There is no higher pleasure than to feel the sway and power of some grand thought, or to be under the spell of some exalted feeling. But this, after all, is the least of the benefits of the coming of the Christ into the life. Many Christians, however, are satisfied with an experience which does not pass this bound. They have the exquisite joy of emotional Christianity, but they have no digestive power. There is no assimilation, no growth, no appearance of new health; there is no change, no development in character. And such experience, such imperfect and inconsistent living, has in the minds of hard-headed and reasoning people brought the Christian life into disrepute. But this is not the Christian life; and this habit is the habit of one who has not in him health of soul. It is the habit of one who lives to eat, and not of one who eats to live; the habit of one who enters into the Christian experience only for the sake of those moments of emotional joy, and not for the sake of reforming his character into the likeness of the Christ.

The real Christian experience carries us beyond these high tides of the spirit. There must be not only a partaking of Christ, but also growth in Christ. This is plainly indicated in

the teaching of Jesus and the Apostles. The
strongest, clearest, and most emphatic words of
Jesus either declare or imply that the Christian
character is a growth. The parable of the sower
represents. the word and the truth of God in
Christ as a seed which is cast into the ground,
which is to spring up, and grow, and bear fruit.
He compares the advancement of the kingdom
of God to the bringing forth of fruit from the
earth, — " first the blade, then the ear, after that
the full corn in the ear." [1] He speaks of himself
as the vine, of the disciples as the branches,[2]
bringing to our minds at once the idea of a
living, organic, growth-producing union between
Christ and the disciples. His life was in them.
They were living, and thriving, and bearing fruit.
Again He uses an emphatic figure of a different
kind, but conveying the same thought. He com-
mands His disciples to eat His flesh and drink
His blood.[3] He declares Himself to be " the
true bread that cometh down from heaven," and
says, "He that eateth me, even he shall live by
me." [4] If these figures do not directly imply
that we are to take the Christ-spirit into our

[1] Mark iv. 28.   [2] John xv. 5.
[3] Ibid. vi. 53.   [4] Ibid. vi. 57.

lives, and digest it, and grow upon it, then they
have no meaning at all. Saint Paul very strongly
conveys the same thought. He uses both the
figure of building and that of growing. He
speaks of God's work through Christ as the perfecting of the saints[1] (even the saints have to
be perfected). He often uses the word "edify,"
which means "building up," and gives us the
idea of a process by which, strength added to
strength, after a time every man is presented
perfect in Christ Jesus.[2] He exhorts the disciples to grow up into Him in all things, who
is the head, even Christ.[3]

Christ, then, must not only enter into the
heart and fill it with splendid sentiment; He
must remain there and feed the moral life.
He must be a constant influence upon the character. Any one can enjoy the Christ for an
hour. It is comparatively easy to have our
hearts stirred on a Sunday by some fervid
word. Most of us are more or less uplifted
by the customary forms of the religious service.
But we have gone only a little way in the religious experience, if this is all. We must feed
upon Christ. We must find Him giving us

[1] Ephesians iv. 12.　[2] Colossians i. 28.　[3] Ephesians iv. 15.

strength. We must see that His spirit is becoming our own. We must feel the glow of health, of spiritual health, and know that we are acquiring moral vigor. We must find in ourselves some greater power to resist evil, some stronger inclination to do good. We must make measurable gains in virtue and purity, in zeal and unselfishness. Can we think that Saint Paul would call any one a good Christian who went on year after year suffering from the very same faults and failings? Could it be justly said that one was growing up into Christ who is just as impatient, just as indifferent, just as selfish now as he was five, ten years ago? The Christians who really exemplify the Christian experience are those whose hearts and minds feed upon Christ, who in all things are enriched by Him,[1] who are created in Christ Jesus unto good works,[2] who, as the years go by, grow more Christlike, more saintly, more pure, more strong.

XI. — RESULTS IN THE INDIVIDUAL.

We consider, next, the results of Christ's work in the life. Perhaps we have trespassed slightly

---

[1] 1 Corinthians i. 5.   [2] Ephesians ii. 10.

upon this ground already, and may seem to have more or less to do with results, in the remainder of the book. But each section has a distinct purpose, and the endeavor will be to make each one serve its special end.

The results of the Christ's work appear in the individual, in society, and in the creation of God. They are found along the lines that radiate from the Christ's character. "We shall be like Him." [1] We may, then, briefly contemplate the Christ, and estimate, so far as is in our power, His moral and spiritual worth.

It is difficult for the human understanding justly to estimate Him, or rightly to describe His character. One undertaking the task seems all the time to be treading on hallowed ground. While he is making the description in human terms, there is something that seems beyond the reach of man-made words. When one thinks he has grasped in some right way the true conception of the Christ, and duly appreciated His worth, there comes a thought of insufficiency, a solemn impression that one is trying to fathom divinity itself. To contemplate the Christ in His moral and spiritual grandeur is to be lifted

[1] 1 John iii. 2.

up above the earth, above all ordinary life, and
to feel the overshadowing of the divine. Hence
the difficulty of putting into human terms all
that He is. We say that He is type of the
highest manhood, — that He is humanity itself
at its height, perfect and complete. He is, as
He most often calls Himself, the " Son of man,"
the perfection of human virtue and grace, en-
shrined in our hearts as our Elder Brother, our
ideal of human excellence.

And yet this is not enough. This does not
compass Jesus the Christ. We feel that there
is more in His life and character than we have
yet told, more than can be measured by these
words. There is in Him a spirit and a power
which cannot be brought down to the level of
the highest flights of the human imagination.
We cannot fully describe Him in terms of human quality and character. In His presence
we rise above the line that marks the limits of
man's aspirations and of the loftiest human
love. We are like one looking into the firma-
ment. *There* is a vision of glory and majesty
that transcends the grandest scenes of the earth.
We are looking out upon the borders and into
the depths of the universe itself. A profound

awe, a sense of the infinite extent, the unknown
depths and heights of the material creation, pos-
sesses us, such as no Alpine grandeur can in-
spire.   We are brought by that upward look
into a new relation with the creation of God.
So it is with the Christ, the Son of man; when
we look earnestly upon His life, we are looking
up into the heavens.   We are in a new presence.
We are looking into the divine depths.   Nothing that our earthly outlook has revealed gives
us the same sense of greatness.   Nothing so im-
presses us with the feeling of the glory and the
beauty and the grandeur of life.   Nothing so takes
our thought and imagination out into a region of
infinite expanse, where is the very essence of
goodness and love.   The Christ carries us out
of ourselves.   He gives the vision of the Divine.
In His presence we are brought into a new
relation with the spiritual creation of God,
with spiritual life, with all morality and truth,
with all righteousness and love.   We are led
up to the Father, and compelled to say, "This
is His beloved Son; this is the Son of
God."

In Christ is the perfect interblending of the
human and the Divine.   He stands at the sum-

mit of human life, and in Him we are lifted up to God.

Christ's work upon and within the human heart bestows and develops those qualities of life which so impress us in Jesus Himself. The man in whose heart the Christ is, is beginning to approach the ideal of human excellence. There is beginning to be in his soul the inter-blending of the human and the Divine. There is something in the Christian life, as in the life of our Lord Himself, that lifts us above the earth, above ourselves, and makes us more sure of God Himself. Every one who heroically and steadfastly obeys the moral law feeds our faith. Every unselfish act affords us a glimpse into heaven. The final outcome of Christ in the life is the man grown into the perfect likeness of Christ. "Whom we preach," says Saint Paul, "warning every man, and teaching every man in all wisdom; that we may present every man perfect in Christ Jesus."[1] "We shall be like Him,"[2] says Saint John; and again Saint Paul, "We all, with open face beholding as in a glass the glory of the Lord, are changed into the same image from glory to glory, even as by the Spirit

[1] Colossians i. 28.   [2] 1 John iii. 2.

of the Lord." [1] " Christ," he says, is " unto us
wisdom, and righteousness, and sanctification,
and redemption;" [2] " Christ in you" is "the hope
of glory." [3] Jesus defines this glory: "Herein is
my Father glorified, that ye bear much fruit;" [4]
and Saint Paul leaves us no doubt as to the nature of the expected fruit: " The fruit of the
spirit is in all goodness and righteousness and
truth." [5] The most glorious and sublime teaching
of all on this point is in the prayer of Jesus
spoken for the help of the disciples in view of
their great trial so soon to come. He prayed
for the very same oneness between Himself and
His present and future disciples as existed between Himself and God: " I in them and thou
in me, that they may be made perfect in one ; " [6]
and says that the glory which God had given
to Him, He has given to those that believe on
His name, " that they may be one," even as He
and the Father are one. This is the consummation of Christ's work in the heart. It is the
man made new in Christ and brought into
Christlike oneness with God.

[1] 2 Corinthians iii. 18.   [2] 1 Corinthians i. 30.
[3] Colossians i. 27.   [4] John xv. 8.
[5] Ephesians v 9.   [6] John xvii. 22, 23.

Regarded by itself, this result may seem like something far removed. It may seem impalpable and in the clouds. We do indeed need to be careful lest we become lost in exalted thought up in a distant region of ideal grace and virtue and glory. We must follow Jesus and the Apostles, and make the work of Christ most present and tangible and real. To those who heard the Christ's words, who received His ministry of love, or listened to His denunciations of wrong, there was nothing sublimated or impractical about Him. We must not depart from His simplicity. We must not be content with rhapsodies over His greatness. When Jesus said, "All things whatsoever ye would that men should do to you, do ye even so to them;"[1] when in the course of that grand discourse on the judgment He said, "Inasmuch as ye have done it unto one of the least of these my brethren, ye have done it unto me;"[2] when He said, "Whosoever shall give unto one of these little ones a cup of cold water only in the name of a disciple . . . he shall in no wise lose his reward;"[3] again, when He prayed for His dis-

[1] Matthew vii. 12. [2] Ibid. xxv. 40.
[3] Ibid. x. 42.

XII. — Results in Society.

further, the results of the Christ's work
in the social organism. The common
hat corporations have no souls indicates
ian work remaining undone. Not till
re social organism has a soul will that
· complete. A renovated society, a di-
ler and life in the earth, was clearly in
ls of the prophets, as the vision of truth
)lded to them. Jesus speaks constantly
ingdom of God, and indicates its growth
:urity in the progress of the earthly gen-
. In fact, He spoke chiefly of that king-
the earth. He describes its manner of
the hindrances it would meet, and its
extent at last.[1] Saint John's ecstatic
as of the New Jerusalem come down to

mnot be satisfied with the state of soci-
ay. We can look back and see that
l.s been large advance along the lines of
·' truth and life. Large and fair portions
· arth have been reclaimed from barba-
)espotism has wellnigh disappeared in
· :he parable of the Mustard seed, the Sower, etc.

ciples, that they should not be taken out of the world but kept from the evil, and that they might be made holy through God's truth,[1] then surely there was nothing distant or obscure or out of reach about His words. We must not become lost in the glory of the final outcome, but must be attentive to the simple results of faithfulness along these practical lines, as they appear in the daily progress of the growing Christian.

The result of the Christ's work in the individual heart is to make him obedient to God, loving, pure, and strong. We can make no statement stronger than Saint Paul's. In the midst of a most practical exhortation to the Ephesians, he announces the great object of the divine ministry in Christ, through apostles, prophets, evangelists, pastors, and teachers, to be " for the perfecting of the saints, unto the work of ministering, unto the building up of the body of Christ: till we all attain unto the unity of the faith, and of the knowledge of the Son of God, *unto a full-grown man, unto the measure of the stature of the fulness of Christ.*"[2]

1 John xvii. 15, 19.
2 Ephesians iv. 12, 13.

XII. — RESULTS IN SOCIETY.

Then, further, the results of the Christ's work appear in the social organism. The common saying that corporations have no souls indicates a Christian work remaining undone. Not till the entire social organism has a soul will that work be complete. A renováted society, a divine order and life in the earth, was clearly in the minds of the prophets, as the vision of truth was unfolded to them. Jesus speaks constantly of the kingdom of God, and indicates its growth and maturity in the progress of the earthly generations. In fact, He spoke chiefly of that kingdom in the earth. He describes its manner of growth, the hindrances it would meet, and its mighty extent at last.[1] Saint John's ecstatic vision was of the New Jerusalem come down to earth.

We cannot be satisfied with the state of society to-day. We can look back and see that there has been large advance along the lines of Christ's truth and life. Large and fair portions of the earth have been reclaimed from barbarism. Despotism has wellnigh disappeared in

[1] See the parable of the Mustard seed, the Sower, etc.

the Christian nations, slavery has been abolished, womanhood has been lifted out of degradation, and brutal warfare has steadily decreased. But when we take in at one view all the wrong and sin and injustice and brutality and selfishness that yet remain, our hearts almost fail us. But as results already have appeared, we have cause to hope and to take courage; and as Christ is in our hearts, we must labor on. The second of the great commandments was not given for naught. " Thou shalt love thy neighbor as thyself " holds a world of meaning. The command has not been sufficiently obeyed. It does not mean that we shall, through neglect or indifference or ignorance, let our neighbor grow up in surroundings that corrupt him body and soul, and then at a late day for the sake of his everlasting welfare send an evangelist to convert him. It does not mean that we shall neglect the children that are growing up cultivated in vice and crime and educated in sin, and then, when sin has already conceived and brought forth death, use all the enginery of the church to drag these poor souls from the brink of an imaginary hell. It does not mean that we shall allow greed and selfishness to make the conditions of human life.

It does not mean that one and another shall feel secure in his individual salvation, and stand passive, while thousands are morally ruined by corrupting circumstances within the control of the Christian's consecrated strength. It means, rather, that Christian spirit shall be thrown into the life of the social order, that Christian love shall be ever working its way into all the channels of life and making itself actively felt. The Christian spirit should be the soul of reforms; it should be making itself felt against every shape of moral disorder. It should be everywhere moulding life and making the conditions of life to its own will and liking. If the Christ-life is in any heart, that one must, like our Lord, be about the Father's work. He who claims to be a Christian and is indifferent to the welfare of his brother-men, has yet the greatest conquest of all to make, the conquest of self. He is far from salvation. "Not every one that saith unto me, Lord, Lord, shall enter into the kingdom of heaven, but he that doeth the will of my Father which is in heaven." [1] "And this is the Father's will, . . . that of all which He hath given me I should lose nothing, but should raise it up again

[1] Matthew vii. 21.

at the last day." [1]   In the process of saving what
God has given to Christ (and the Father hath
given all things into His hands),[2] the Second Com-
mandment plays an important part.   There must
come, through the Christian love of men one for
another, a better order of life, a better society,
more favorable to the culture of virtue, better
adapted to produce the highest types of manhood and womanhood, in which shall be the
minimum of injustice and oppression and wrong,
in which the Christian influence shall be a larger
power, and all the conditions of living more
favorable to Christian culture.   Individualism is
the dry rot of the Christian life.   Each Christian is not a whole, but a unit of a whole, — members in particular, but the body of Christ.   " By
one spirit are we all baptized into one body." [3]
The strong tendency in Christianity has been to
individualism.   A reaction has come, and the
touch of the Christ is now more firmly felt upon
the general life of the day.

The time must come when the world will be
blessed with a society organized upon a Christian basis.   This is one of the necessary results

---

[1] John vi. 39.   [2] Ibid. iii. 35.
[3] 1 Corinthians xii. 13, 20, 27.

of the indwelling of Christ in the life. "The future is lighted up with the radiant colors of hope. Strife and sorrow shall disappear. Peace and love shall reign supreme. The dream of poets, the lesson of priest and prophet, the inspiration of the great musician" shall be realized. "And as we gird ourselves up for the work of life, we may look forward to the time when in the truest sense the kingdoms of the world shall become the kingdom of Christ, and He shall reign forever and ever, king of kings and lord of lords."[1]

XIII. — RESULTS IN THE CREATION OF GOD.

The results of the Christ's work appear, further, in the creation of God.

The Christ's work has no limit of time or place. It is not confined to this earth or to the physical existence of man. He preaches to spirits in prison in the bondage of disobedience, wherever they are. Grand as seems the work of perfecting the individual soul or of renewing the human society on earth, the work of the Christ is infinitely larger and grander than that. It is God's saving and renewing work in all His

[1] Destiny of Man, by John Fiske, pp. 118, 119.

creation. Christ is God pushing Himself out to the farthest bounds of His creation ; God reaching and permeating all life ; God strengthening the weak, renewing that which was impaired, perfecting the imperfect, completing the incomplete, imparting Himself and His glory to all the universe. "The Father loveth the Son," said John the Baptist, "and hath given all things into His hand." [1] To the Christ is committed not only the care of this little planet and its people, but of all the creation of God. We cannot have a sufficient reverence for the Christ, unless we realize how much God has intrusted to Him and how much He expects of Him. He gave all things into His hands. "All that the Father hath," He said, "are mine." "All that the Father giveth to me shall come to me; and him that cometh to me I will in no wise cast out." [2] Nothing less than this perfect completion of the Christ's work was in the minds of the Apostles. Saint John says that "the Son of God was manifested that He might destroy the works of the devil." [3] All that is evil, all that is opposed to God, is summed up and personified in the word "devil." This the Christ

[1] John iii. 35.   [2] Ibid. vi. 37.   [3] 1 John iii. 8.

is sent to destroy. Saint Paul states the fact from the positive side, saying that God had made known the mystery of His will, which He had purposed in Himself, " that in the dispensation of the fulness of times He might gather together in one all things in Christ, both which are in heaven and which are on earth." [1] He says, in plain and unmistakable terms, " the creation itself also shall be delivered from the bondage of corruption into the liberty of the glory of the children of God ;" [2] and he gives us that splendid picture of the consummation, which has not been surpassed: " Then cometh the end, when He [the Christ] shall have put down all rule and all authority and power. For He must reign till He hath put all enemies under His feet. . . . And when all things shall be subdued unto Him, then shall the Son also Himself be subject unto Him that put all things under Him, that God may be all in all." [3] " There is no power to come forth out from the beginning or the end, from the first to the last, with intimations of force or fear, that can . . . effect the

---

[1] Ephesians i. 9, 10.
[2] Romans viii. 21 (Revised Version).
[3] 1 Corinthians xv. 24–28.

subversion of the love that is at the source and centre of all things, or the disruption of the unity that is in the will of God, that is manifesting itself in the reconciliation of all things. The Christ says, 'I know whence I came and whither I go ;' and again, 'I am the first and the last, the beginning and the end; I am he that was, and is, and is to come.' "[1] The work of the Christ is not complete, it cannot be ended, it will not cease, till God is all in all. All things are given into the hands of the beloved Son, and nothing shall be lost. Creation shall be delivered from its bondage. The glory of God, which is the fruit of the Spirit in all goodness and righteousness and truth, shall reach to the outermost bounds of the universe, and God's will in Christ be done. There will be no more rebellion, no more disobedience, no more weakness of spirit and will, no more evil, no more sin, but God shall have given His life through Christ to all. At the name of Jesus every knee shall bow with reverence and glad joy, and every tongue make haste to confess that the Christ is Lord to the glory of God the Father.[2]

[1] Mulford's Republic of God, pp. 180, 181.
[2] Philippians ii. 11.

Such is the result of the Christ's work in the creation of God. Is it not blessed that behind the solemn and oppressive mystery of the universe lies this great thought? When for the moment we are looking off into the darkness, hushed by the silence, feeling the mighty grandeur and the infinite power all about us, crying out perhaps with the Psalmist, " What is man that thou art mindful of him?" — when it all seems too great for our understanding, and this great theatre of life and action, limited only by the bounds which shut in the stars, oppresses us with a sense of our own littleness and ignorance, — is it not blessed that then out from the darkness, out from the fathomless depths, stream rays of glorious light? Is it not blessed that there are such lines of illumination across all this mystery, and we are assured that there lies in the soundless depths an Infinite love, a Father's thought and care? No greater thought can possess us, and none can be the source of a deeper content and peace, than that the Infinite Being wills to His creation only good. Nothing can more touch the heart and lift up the voice in glad praise than to know that the Almighty Spirit of this great universe is swayed by love, and that all creation

shall share the blessings of that love through
the redeeming and renewing work of the Son
of God.

XIV. — TESTS OF THE CHRISTIAN LIFE.

It is to be remembered that we are treating a
practical theme in a practical way. We want
the Christian life. We want to use every means
to that end that God has placed in our hands.
We want by help of these means to come near
to Christ and to grow in Christian character.
We desire that results appear. Now, there are
certain tests which will indicate whether or not
we are gaining the desired end. There is an
inclination to neglect the tests. The beginnings
of religious life have had the most attention.
Greater effort has been made to convert sinners
than to cultivate saints. More energy and zeal
have been thrown into the work of conversion
than into rigorous training in the Christian way.
It has been at the cost of strength and life.
Christian work has too often stopped at a point
not far beyond the beginning. If tests have
been applied, it has not been in the wholesome
way indicated by Saint John in his First Epistle.
He who has come within the Christian influence

has not been moved to inquire, "How much progress am I making in Christian life?" but rather to ask, "Am I saved?" The popular mind has dwelt far more on the beginnings than on the progress of the Christian life. The people have been more concerned about conversion and salvation from future suffering and woe than about abiding in the vine and bearing much fruit. This has been a natural effect of the doctrine of salvation commonly held, and of the old revival system. The tests of Saint John, which will be stated, have not been sufficiently applied. The great object of Christian experience, the one special and supreme end, in the popular way of thinking, is gained at the very outset. That gained, it is easy to lapse back into indifference, or to make Christian disciples of the weakest sort. But the neglect of the tests is not wholly due to doctrinal teaching. It is a general failing. We do not like to square up our conduct with the highest standards. We do not like to trouble ourselves with the vigorous work which alone can show where we stand and what we are. It disturbs our ease and peace to take a thorough-going inventory of ourselves.

We ought not to be indifferent to the develop-

ment of Christian character. We must learn to
identify this work with salvation. Salvation is
character-building. There are tests by which
we may know whether or not we have the Christian spirit or are making Christian progress.
There are connected with the great revivals what
are called inquiry-rooms. A frequent question
there is, " Are you a Christian?" It is a good
question, and we ought to be able to give some
sensible and reasonable answer. But the answer
should not signify merely a profession or non-
profession of faith. It should tell of the life.
It should make known the motives, the word,
and the act. It should search the heart, and
make known what is found. It should go
deep into the soul, and inform us what is there.
It would be well for the whole Christian world,
all church-members, all members of congrega-
tions, to hear the question, " Are you a Christian?" To answer it intelligently would be a
good healthy exercise, and fruitful perhaps in
good results. And the inquiry cannot be better
directed than by the Apostle John. He says in
his First Epistle : " Hereby we do know that we
know Him, *if we keep His commandments.*" [1]

---

[1] 1 John ii. 3.

" Whoso keepeth His word, in him verily is the
love of God perfected : hereby know we that we
are in Him. He that saith he abideth in Him
ought himself also so to walk, even as He walked."[1]
These would be good words for the inquiry-
room. These are good words for the Christian
world. These are tests of the Christian life. Are
we following Christ? Are we walking, as He
walked? Are we keeping the commandments?
But Saint John is still more explicit. We ask,
perhaps, What is it to keep the commandments,
what is it to follow in Christ's footsteps? One
need not read far in Saint John's Epistle before
he will get full information. " He that saith
he is in the light, and hateth his brother, is in
darkness even until now. He that loveth his
brother abideth in the light."[2] This is one of
the easiest and most quickly applied tests. It
is equivalent to asking : What is your spirit
toward the world? Are you selfish or have you
the spirit of Christ? This is a searching question, a thorough-going test. But it must be
applied. Then Saint John says again: " If ye
know that He is righteous, ye know that every
one that doeth righteousness is born of Him."[3]

[1] 1 John ii. 5, 6.   [2] Ibid. ii. 9, 10.   [3] Ibid. ii. 29.

Here is more light. We distinguish right from wrong. We know what it is to do right. Does one want to know whether he is really a Christian, let him ask himself, "Do I love righteousness always and everywhere, in every form, in every shape? Am I striving with all my might to do right to the best of my knowledge and ability, and after the example of Christ?" "In this the children of God are manifest, and the children of the devil: whosoever doeth not righteousness is not of God, neither he that loveth not his brother." [1]

But we want to push the inquiry still further. One may say, "I love my brother man." But he may be pertinently asked: "How much do you love your fellow-men? What evidence is there of your love? Is it a sentiment that you enjoy all to yourself? Do you sit by your comfortable fireside of a winter's night, and weep mawkish tears over those who are shivering in cold garrets? Do you enjoy your luxuries and comforts, and content yourself with wishing that every one could be so blessed?" If so one loves his fellow-men, it is befitting that he study Saint John's word. "Hereby know we love, because

[1] 1 John iii. 10.

He laid down His life for us; and we ought to lay down our lives for the brethren."[1] How can we lay down our lives for the brethren? We are not called to the stake to meet a martyr's death. We have to endure no persecution. But some words of Saint John signify how we may lay down our lives. "Whoso hath the world's goods, and beholdeth his brother in need, and shutteth up his compassion from him, how doth the love of God abide in him? My little children, let us not love in word, neither with the tongue; but in deed and truth."[2] If we see our brother have need, there is the opportunity and then comes the test. Saint James puts it even more strongly: "If a brother or sister be naked, and destitute of daily food, and one of you say unto them, Depart in peace, be ye warmed and filled; notwithstanding ye give them not those things which are needful to the body; what doth it profit?"[3] Jesus said, "By their fruits ye shall know them;"[4] and again, "Ye are my friends, if ye do whatsoever I command you."[5] And the splendid lesson of the parable of the sheep and the goats must not be forgotten. Je-

[1] 1 John iii. 16.   [2] Ibid. iii. 17, 18.   [3] James ii. 15, 16.
[4] Matthew vii. 20.   [5] John xv. 14.

sus there said that the righteous inherited the
kingdom of heaven; that it was prepared for
them from the foundation of the world; that it
was theirs because "I was an hungred, and ye
gave me meat: I was thirsty, and ye gave me
drink: I was a stranger, and ye took me in:
naked, and ye clothed me: I was sick, and ye
visited me: I was in prison, and ye came unto
me." [1]   Astonished beyond measure, the right-
eons say: "Lord, when saw we thee an hungred, and fed thee? or thirsty, and gave thee
drink?   When saw we thee a stranger, and took
thee in? or naked, and clothed thee? or when
saw we thee sick, or in prison, and came unto
thee?" [1]   And the answer was, "Inasmuch as ye
have done it unto one of the least of these my
brethren, ye have done it unto me." [1]

Such tests are ready to our hand.   They have
been neglected.   Life has not been brought vig-
orously to the Christian standard.   It has been
a misfortune that salvation has in the popular
mind been identified with conversion rather
than with growth in Christian character, and
that prevailing doctrines and methods have
made it so easy to get the impression that

[1] Matthew xxv. 35–40.

Christ's work in and for us was completed in the emotional experience of an hour. There is need of emphatic teaching that there is no genuine Christian life without constant obedience, and that salvation is only attained by the growth of the soul into the likeness of Christ. The application of these tests, then, is commended. They are Christian tests. They are from Paul and Peter and James and John, and from our Lord Himself. There can be no better religious exercise than to take such passages as have been freely quoted in this section, and make them daily companions of the thought, and, while we inquire after the welfare of our souls, let them be as a lamp unto our feet and a light unto our path. Nothing could be more wholesome for the whole Christian world than to pause in the midst of its activities, and apply these tests with conscientious vigor to its life.

"Every one that loveth is born of God, and knoweth God. He that loveth not knoweth not God; for God is love." [1] "If we love one another, God dwelleth in us, and His love is perfected in us." [2] "If a man say, I love God, and hateth his brother, he is a liar: for

[1] 1 John iv. 7, 8.   [2] Ibid. iv. 12.

he that loveth not his brother whom he hath
seen, how can he love God whom he hath not
seen." [1]

XV. — INCENTIVES TO THE CHRISTIAN LIFE.

Are there any statements that may be made,
any facts that may be presented, as incentives to
the Christian life? Of course there are many
good reasons why one ought to live in discipleship of Christ; but waiving the question of duty
we ask now, What is there to invite one to become a follower of Christ?

There is just one powerful incentive, and that
is the intrinsic worth and attractiveness of the
Christian life itself. There is no better way to
move quickly and deeply those not yet inter-
ested in the Lord Jesus than to present to them
the Christian life as it is. No stronger incentive
can be held forth.

For some reason there is a wide-spread false
impression with regard to the Christian life.
There are many outside the Church who either
have no idea at all of what that life is, or
else have a wretchedly false conception. Many
people think of a Christian as one who stoops

[1] 1 John iv. 20.

as he walks, who drawls his words, seldom smiles, is punctiliously pious, and terribly exacting; whom nobody loves, and few can get along with; whose family do not enjoy him; who quarrels with his church, but is always there, and exhorts and prays. Of course there are such pious hypocrites, whose religion is less than skin-deep; and so this travesty on the Christian character has taken a firm hold upon those who have no great love of the Church or any of its belongings, and through them spreads its poison and does a vast amount of harm. It is a great pity that there is such an idea afloat. It is a great pity that in so many cases this false idea supersedes all others. But it is no wonder that the Christian life is not attractive to those who thus understand it.

Perhaps the Church itself is partly in fault for the spread of this false idea. Not that the Church has ever presented such a type of Christian character as its ideal, but it has neglected to show up in its true colors the genuine attractiveness of the Christian life. The emphasis of its teaching has been elsewhere. The intrinsic merit and worth of the Christian character have not been dwelt upon. The Christian experience has been set forth, not as grand and desirable in itself, but as a means of gaining heaven. It would be a gross slander to say that the Church has not inculcated a high morality, and sought to make the life conform to the example of Christ. But the hope of heaven has been the main thought. It has engrossed the popular ear; it has been so ingrained into theology, and so possessed the mind, that doubtless to-day the majority of devout Christians think more about their religion as something that will do them a great good after they die than as something to make them fit to live here on earth before they die, and are more anxious about getting to heaven than concerned to love their neighbors as themselves. The common teaching has strongly tended to identify the emotional experience of an hour with the fulness and sufficiency of the Christian life. In this way the religious life has been made to appear something vastly less than what it really is. Christ's virtue and manhood have not been held up before men. A feeling grows up that heaven is cheaply secured. The main lines of Christian teaching hitherto followed do not, as they ought, connect every act, every thought, every throb of the

heart with the life that Christ would have us,
live, but tend rather to produce a feeling that
the lapses of the moment, the selfishness, of
to-day, the sin by the fireside or in the counting-
room are not of any special account, because
salvation is already secured.

Thus the Christian life has not been strongly
presented to men for its own sake and in the
light of its intrinsic worth. When it is so
presented its attractiveness will appear. No
stronger, no higher incentive can be held up
before one not yet committed to Christ, than
just to picture the Christian life as it is. We
must trust in the simple and grand worth of
the life itself. We must publish it abroad and
glory in its noble attributes.

The qualities that go to make up the Christian
are those which we cannot help admiring. We
cannot refuse our homage to Jesus of Nazareth
or to His genuine and faithful followers. The
rankest infidel may be defied to withhold his
admiration from a whole-souled noble Christian.
The secularist himself makes up his ideal of
manhood out of the very qualities that enter into
the Christian life. God never made anything
more grand than a Christian heart; and every-

body has to confess it, everybody feels it. There is something in the Christian character which we cannot refuse to see, and, seeing, we cannot refuse to love. It has a worth and glory of its own. It controls and directs in its own way, invisibly and silently and yet with irresistible power, all the thought and love of man. That character permeating the life of the ages is like the great magnetic earth current. As every magnetic needle must swing at the behest of that great current, and though it vacillate and quiver under many shocks, must at last point to the pole; so human love must swing toward the Christian life, and though under a thousand shocks it vacillate and quiver and point momentarily in this direction or that, it must at last come to its rest pointed steadfastly toward Christ.

There is something inherently and of necessity attractive in the Christian life. The great need is to make men know that life in its real worth. Show them how grand it is, and how poor is the life that has not the Christian quality. We have confidently, continuously, earnestly, trustingly, and in the power of the Spirit, to present the Christ as He is, to make Him appear before the

world in His own glory. This must be the
sufficient incentive to the Christian life. And,
be it deliberately said, if this cannot, then nothing can attract men helpfully to Jesus the Christ,
or move them to become His followers and
loyal disciples.

XVI. — REWARDS OF THE CHRISTIAN LIFE.

Lastly, the Christian experience has its ample
rewards. These rewards are not to be urged as
supplying motive; they crown the life. He who
labors for them loses them. If the rewards become an object of effort, they are sure to be
missed. The rewards are certain states of the
heart and mind, bringing peace and joy; they
are the results of genuine Christian life; they
cannot be had without the unclouded Christian
heart, — the pure, unselfish motive. He who is
honest because honesty is the best policy is not
an honest man. The very statement implies a
lack of genuine honor. If dishonesty were the
best policy, then he would be dishonest. He
who does his neighbor a kindness in order that
he may go home and ruminate upon his own
goodness is a selfish man, and is by his selfishness debarred from the rewards of the Christian.

He who conforms to certain prescribed conditions solely for the purpose of gaining a happy hereafter is working from selfish motives. Though he may take great satisfaction in the thought that his future is secure, he is far from having the true Christian's reward. If one would know the nature of the reward, he must come into intimacy with Jesus, — he must come into that frame of mind, that fulness of heart, which will enable him to appreciate the beatitudes of our Lord; he must know something of the happiness of the poor in spirit, of the meek, of those who do hunger and thirst after righteousness, of the merciful, of the pure in heart, of the peacemakers, of those who are persecuted for righteousness' sake. The great reward is the possession of the mind and spirit of Christ.

The rewards are indicated in the words of Jesus and the Apostles, and illustrated by the glimpses that we have of their own inner life. They are vastly different from the rewards of ordinary effort. We have made ourselves largely dependent upon our material surroundings, and demand as the condition of happiness favoring circumstances. Jesus and the Apostles made

themselves largely independent of material surroundings, and their happiness was conditioned
upon no outward circumstance whatever. The
Pharisees sought the reward of right-doing in
the enjoyment of a certain reputation among their
fellows. They prayed and fasted and gave alms
to be seen of men. Such a reward was very un-
certain and unsatisfactory ; for it was subject to
the caprice and jealousy of the whole group who
were aiming to establish a reputation for piety.
Thieves could easily steal this reputation, and
make valueless this ostentatious fasting and
praying and giving. But Jesus speaks of the
rewards of the private prayer, of unostentatious
fasting, of giving alms with the right hand without the knowledge of the left. These are the
true rewards ; these are treasures laid up in
heaven, " where neither moth nor rust doth corrupt, and where thieves do not break through
nor steal." [1]

We get a good idea of these rewards when we
look upon our Lord in those moments when
there was nothing left to Him but Himself and
His Father in heaven. Then, though He was
human and suffered most intensely in a very

[1] Matthew vi. 20.

human way, there was above and around and
beneath and through His sufferings a deep peace
and joy. In all the final struggle, which was indeed a sore trial to Him, there was yet a calm, a
repose of spirit, a consciousness of God's presence, a trust, a hope, a faith, that were His pos-
sessions, His own all the time. When at one time
the burden of the moment seemed too heavy,
and He inquired within Himself whether He
should say, "Father, save me from this hour,"
He met this thought with a greater, — "For this
cause came I unto this hour." [1] In Gethsemane,
at the trials, on Calvary, there is evidence of the
strength of His life, — evidence that He had
treasures in His heart and soul of which He was
not deprived even in ignominy and death. He
found His sufficient strength and joy in the consciousness that He was obeying the Divine law
and carrying out the Divine will. "To this end
was I born, and for this cause came I into the
world," He said to Pilate, "that I should bear
witness unto the truth." We can learn something
about His sublime faith, and of its great worth
to Him, and of how there was reward for His
steadfastness and for His life of trial and suffer-

[1] John xii. 27.

ing, when we hear Him before the Roman governor, a prisoner in chains, already condemned, and under the very shadow of the cross, calmly saying, "Every one that is of the truth heareth my voice." [1]

Saint Paul, it must be briefly said, gloriously presents to us the splendid rewards of the Christian life. To be familiar with his record, and to supplement that record with his epistles, is to know what strength of soul, fulness of spirit, and a heart that loves God and man, can do for one who has sacrificed every worldly ambition and gone out to a bitter struggle, to a life of toil and danger and deprivation, in order to establish Christ's truth in the earth. We have only to know of his toils and perils, of his bitter contests with Jew and Pagan, to remember that he suffered imprisonment and stripes, was beaten and stoned, and then to turn to his words, "God hath revealed unto us by the Spirit" "the things which God hath prepared for them that love Him," [2] to hear him crying out, "Oh the depth of the riches both of the wisdom and knowledge of God;" [3] to hear him calmly

[1] John xviii. 37.　　[2] 1 Corinthians ii. 9, 10.
[3] Romans xi. 33.

asserting that he is troubled on every side yet not distressed, perplexed but not in despair, persecuted but not forsaken, cast down but not destroyed, and declaring that in the midst of all that was adverse to and destructive of the joys and prosperity of the outward man, he was renewed and strengthened in spirit day by day,[1] and that for this cause he fainted not, and that all his sufferings seemed light because he was looking upon the unseen and eternal truths of God, and living for them, and not for the seen and temporal,[2] or, as we might say, not for the express and only purpose of being well fed, well clothed, well housed, and provided with all the material comforts that wealth can buy, — we have only to know and appreciate these facts in Saint Paul's life to be amply informed with regard to the rewards of the Christian experience.

We are not offered wealth nor any material thing, but something far more substantial and enduring. Wealth cannot give it to us, nor can wealth take it away when once it is ours. Calamity and sorrow do not furnish it, nor can calamity and sorrow deprive us of it. It is that

[1] 2 Corinthians, iv. 8, 9, 16.　　[2] Ibid. 17, 18.

breadth and depth of spirit and life which is the one constant force within us through every experience. To gain that is to be in fellowship with Christ, and to have a reward above all price.

Conclusion.

We have written of Christ in the Life: of the reality of Christ; of what hinders His work in our hearts and in the world; of what helps us to receive His spirit and to live by it; of our close and brotherly relation with our Lord, whereby we feel the touch of His spirit with ours; of Christian growth unto the fulness of His stature; of the results of the Redeemer's work; of the tests of the Christian life; of its incentives, and of its rewards.

One question remains to be asked. To it each one should give answer. Not to answer is almost as much a sin as to answer wrongly. The question is this: Will you learn of Christ and have Him in your life? Upon our answer to that question depends the worth of our lives to ourselves and to the world. These are days when one needs to live with eyes wide open. A hundred catchpenny thoughts and notions are afloat.　We are beset with a style of life that puts spurs to false ambitions.　The scales in which we weigh values are out of gear.　They are telling off to the world that nothing has worth that does not clink in the balance.　They have been so tampered with that they do not indicate the worth of righteousness and truth and love.　In the midst of the error and sin of the world there is just one saving power, — *the divine life in us, and in us as it was in Christ.* That is an everlasting fact, — "the same yesterday, to-day, and forever."　"This is the record, that God hath given to us eternal life, and this life is in His Son."[1]　That fact no argument has touched.　The storms of severest criticism have beat upon it, but it has stood.　The outposts of the Christian position have been many times built upon the sands, and the floods of criticism have come, and the winds of earnest thought have blown, and the outworks have fallen ; but the citadel, the strong fortress of our Lord, the everlasting fact that the divine life as it is in Christ is the world's saving power, has stood unshaken, founded on the rock.　This fortress needs no defence.　It wants nothing at our

[1] 1 John v. 11.

hands. It is our defence, our stronghold. Its strength may become our strength. It will furnish the vantage-ground of our life.

The times demand earnest living. The youth of to-day — the young men and young women, who are taking their places as citizens, as business men, as guardians of homes; who are coming on to fill the innumerable places in the schools, in the shops, in the professions, in every calling and every station of life — have glorious opportunities before them, and serious duties and responsibilities are laid upon them. If they yield to the temptations that wait to deceive and entrap them, if they are drawn into the purely mercenary and selfish style of life or into the ways of passion and sin, they may know that they are spreading destruction all about. They are working evil upon themselves; they are doing harm to their neighbors and to the world.

While, if their eyes are opened to see, and they learn to note how hideous are passion and sin, into what awfulness of degradation the transgression of the law of God sinks its victims, how selfishness is the handmaid of sin, and how the mercenary spirit eats out the best part of the soul, then are they in such mood as will bring them near to Christ. And if, further, they take Christ into their hearts and carry the Christian spirit into trade, into the home, into citizenship, everywhere into all the walks and avenues of life, then are they ministering to their own highest welfare, giving help and life to the world, establishing God's kingdom and doing His will in earth as it is done in heaven.

Cambridge: John Wilson & Son, University Press.

Lightning Source UK Ltd.
Milton Keynes UK
UKHW022207021218
333278UK00006B/530/P